THE
Ahwahnee
HOTEL

by Shirley Sargent

Yosemite
National Park

Centennial
1990

Produced for Yosemite Park & Curry Co.
by Sequoia Communications
Santa Barbara, California

Coordination by John Graham
Edited by Nicky Leach
Designed by Adine Maron
Type by Graphic Traffic, Santa Barbara
Printed in Hong Kong by Everbest/Asia Print

ISBN (pbk): 0-917859-38-3
ISBN (hdbk): 0-917859-39-1
Library of Congress No. 90-070052

ILLUSTRATION CREDITS

New photography by *Jeff Brouws* on the following pages: Title spread, 5, 10, 23, 24, 25, 26, 31 (right), 43 (bottom), 58-59, 60 (top), 61 (top), 62 (middle), 62-63 (top), and rug and architectural details throughout.

Ansel Adams, Shirley Sargent Collection: 41, 42; *Ansel Adams, Yosemite Park & Curry Co. Collection:* 22 (bottom), 28, 30, 31 (top left), 40, 44, 46; *Dick Connett:* 33; *Dewitt Jones:* 8-9, 38-39, 43 (top), 45, 61 (bottom), 62 (top left), back cover; *A.G. Kulisch:* 17; *National Park Service, Grand Canyon National Park:* 11 (bottom); *National Park Service, Yellowstone National Park:* 11 (top); *National Park Service, Yosemite Collections:* 12 (bottom), 13, 14 (top), 15, 16 (top), 18-19, 35, 36, 37 (bottom), 47, 48-49, 51 (courtesy of Joseph C. Lellig Collection), 54-55; *Nebraska Historical Society:* 17; *Jeff Nicholas:* cover; *Shirley Sargent Collection:* 12 (top), 14 (bottom), 15, 16 (bottom), 32, 37 (top left, right), 52, 53, 55 (right), 56; *Yosemite Park & Curry Co. Collection:* IFC-1, 6, 20, 21, 22 (top), 27, 31 (bottom left), 57, 60 (bottom), 62 (bottom right), 64-IBC; *Ann Underwood:* 17; *Steve Whittaker:* 62 (bottom left).

Acknowledgements

We would like to thank the following people for their assistance with this book: Yosemite Park & Curry Co. executives Ed Hardy, President; John Graham, Vice President, Retail; and John Poimiroo, Vice President of Communications; Nancy Tilson, Assistant, Marketing; Linda Eade, Librarian, Yosemite National Park Research Library; David Forgang, Curator, National Park Service, Yosemite Collections; Hank Johnston for his editorial review of the text. The author also wishes to thank Dayle Law and Nicky Leach for their help in typing the manuscript.

CONTENTS

CHAPTER I
A Hotel for all Seasons

T he story goes that one spring in the 1920s,
American-born Lady Astor, England's first
female member of parliament and one of the
most important women of her day, registered at the
venerable Sentinel Hotel in Yosemite Valley. After a
horrified look at the drafty, unheated room and the
communal bath at the end of the hall, she checked out
and swept off in her chauffeured limousine. When
Stephen T. Mather, director of the National Park Service,
heard of her slight to his beloved Yosemite National
Park, he determined that the time had come for the
aging Sentinel to be replaced by a first-class hotel.

Whether the story is true or not, it is a fact that on July
14, 1927, Mather proudly presided at the opening of a
year-round, luxury hotel in Yosemite Valley named The
Ahwahnee that, to this day, is one of America's most
beautifully integrated examples of what is known as
Rustic architecture.

Mather's push for better services and attractive accommodations in Yosemite and the nation's other national
parks had several purposes. The National Park Service,
created in 1916, was still struggling for congressional
funding. If facilities in the parks were improved enough

Previous page: The Ahwahnee subtly blends into its natural environment of granite and trees, especially in winter.

A detail from the ornate mural in the writing room of The Ahwahnee. Painted by Robert Boardman Howard, it colorfully intermingles the flora and fauna of Yosemite. Howard was heavily influenced by the decorative work of William Morris and the British Arts and Crafts movement.

to encourage greater public interest in visiting them, Mather and his assistant Horace Albright reasoned, it would be easier to obtain increased funding for the National Park Service and the park system. A more sympathetic public would do much to gain support for preservation of America's wild places through legislation and funding.

In the early twenties, the proliferation of automobiles and the post-World War I boom resulted in expanded tourism and a need for more and better roads and accommodations throughout the country. America was on the move. Grand hotels went up, particularly in scenic resort areas. It was an era of entrepreneurs, high style, and attention to detail. Hotels offered the all-inclusive "American Plan" and actively encouraged families to check in for extended stays.

RUSTIC ARCHITECTURE

Mather's development of an extensive building plan for the parks was a pet project. He and Albright had given a lot of thought to the type of architecture appropriate to the natural splendor of the national preserves. In the late teens, while the National Park Service was in its infancy, they had toured the nation's parks and admired buildings such as Old Faithful Inn in Yellowstone National Park and El Tovar Hotel at the South Rim of the Grand Canyon that blended appropriately with the environment. They felt that this type of "environmental" architecture fit in well with the overwhelming majesty of the national parks.

Rustic architecture, which began to be popular in this country at the turn of the century, sought to integrate buildings unobtrusively with the environment by the use of scale appropriate to the surroundings and rough, natural materials. It had its roots in the British Arts and Crafts movement of the 1880s, when a group that came to be known as the Pre-Raphaelites rejected the increasingly soulless life of the industrialized cities and fled back to nature in the British countryside.

The movement's leader, William Morris, created an artistic community that encouraged the pursuit of all the arts, and specialized in the manufacture of furniture, fabrics, and self-published booklets reflecting the views of the group's participants. The Medieval Gothic era was their inspiration.

Joyce Zaitlin in her book, *Gilbert Stanley Underwood: His Rustic, Art Deco, and Federal Architecture,* writes: "... these design elements were readily adopted by romantic Americans and the NPS.... as writer Harvey L. Jones has pointed out, 'American sensibility formed by the puritan work ethic and background of pioneer experiences readily accepted the aesthetic principles which extended from the English Arts and Crafts movement of the 1880s.' It fit in, too, with the American longing to return to its pioneer past. *The Craftsman,* an American magazine inspired by William Morris's ideas, played an important role in promoting handicrafts, in placing importance on American Indian designs and crafts, as well as in popularizing Rustic architecture." By the early

20th century, the stage was set for a new type of environmentally conscious, luxurious lodging to be constructed in the nation's national parks.

YOSEMITE'S ANCIENT SETTLERS

The area on the bank of the Merced River just west of Royal Arches, which was eventually chosen to become The Ahwahnee hotel, had been used for centuries as a summer encampment by a band of Miwok Indians calling themselves the Ah-wah-ni-chis. This encampment was one of 37 campsites inhabited by the Native Americans in the valley they called *Ah-wah-ni* or "large, gaping mouth."

The site afforded spectacular views of several of Yosemite's most dramatic landmarks—Half Dome, Glacier Point, and Royal Arches. The Native Americans lived in peaceful harmony with the naturally sheltered environment. They respected the valley and found significance in its dramatic granite features. To them, the whole natural world was imbued with spirits and everything had its place in the natural order.

This peaceful way of life was disrupted in the middle of the nineteenth century by the first white pioneers to venture deep into the craggy Sierra Nevada. Many had traveled west in pursuit of fame and fortune after the discovery of gold at Sutter's Mill in northern California.

The foothills west of Yosemite Valley attracted hundreds of prospectors who, truly, "struck it rich." They dammed creeks and rivers, killed herds of deer and

Old Faithful Inn, Yellowstone National Park (top), designed by Robert Reamer in 1903, and El Tovar Hotel, South Rim, Grand Canyon National Park (above), designed by Charles Whittlesley in 1904, were early examples of rustic architecture admired by NPS Director Stephen Mather and his assistant, Horace Albright.

other wildlife, and cut down the trees for timber. In addition, they accorded little respect to the Native American people they found in the area and engaged in wanton rape and killing of its population.

The relationship between the Native Americans and white settlers deteriorated to the extent that Indians began to stage retaliatory raids on the miners and pioneer outposts. In 1851, a vengeful trader named James Savage formed the Mariposa Battalion of 204 volunteers, authorized by the governor of California, and headed deep into the Sierra where many Indians had fled. The party was only partly successful in its attempt to capture the shrewd native people, but one of the companies did succeed in entering the valley. The men promptly began to name the valley and its granite features. Lafayette H. Bunnell, a 27-year-old member of the company, was responsible for the valley's present name, calling it Yo-sem-i-ty under the mistaken belief that this was the Indians' name for it.

In 1855, unconfirmed reports of the towering granite rocks and pleasant, verdant valley below inspired four parties of miners and tourists to visit Yosemite. The first group was led by an English journalist, James Mason Hutchings, who fell in love with the valley, wrote eloquently of its beauty, and returned later to manage what ultimately became the first unit of the Sentinel Hotel. Thomas Ayres, the artist in the party, recorded Yosemite's scenic wonders for an incredulous public.

Top: Lafayette H. Bunnell entered Yosemite Valley with the Mariposa Battalion in 1851. Bunnell named the valley Yosemite, believing that was the local Indian name for it. Galen Clark later wrote that he understood Yosemite to be the Indians' name for their group, a branch of the Ahwahnichi. Above: This view of Yosemite by photographer Carleton Watkins was instrumental in persuading Congress to enact the Yosemite Grant of 1864.

Yosemite Valley was almost immediately popular. It was not long before homesteading and tourism began to wreak havoc on its fragile ecological balance. In 1864, the efforts of I. W. Raymond, a San Francisco shipping executive, and other influential people helped create the landmark Yosemite Grant. Under it, Yosemite Valley and the Mariposa Grove of Big Trees were given to the State of California by the federal government as a scenic preserve.

In 1890, 18 years after the establishment of Yellowstone National Park (the first park under federal jurisdiction), and largely through the efforts of John Muir and his powerful ally, Century Magazine editor Robert Underwood Johnson, Yosemite National Park came into being. It protected 1,500 square miles of the Sierra Nevada surrounding the Yosemite Valley Grant. In 1906, after it became apparent that the Grant was still inadequately protected against overuse, Muir was again largely responsible for the receding of the Yosemite Grant to become part of the better-protected national park.

PIONEERING INNKEEPERS ON THE MERCED

The area that is now home to The Ahwahnee hotel continued to be a popular site. In 1878, Aaron Harris began a private campground west of the original Native American camp, which had dwindled in population as more and more white visitors settled the valley. Harris's Royal Arch Farm included a store and a dairy and lasted about 10 years.

In 1885, Harris gained a neighbor to his east. During that year,

Top: This 1872 photograph by Edweard Muybridge shows the Ahwahnichi after contact with the white man. Left: Naturalist and Yosemite booster John Muir, circa 1910.

13

A Hotel for All Seasons

William Coffman and George Kenney combined their rival horse-and-mule businesses into Coffman and Kenney and set up business, which eventually occupied 15 buildings near the base of Royal Arches. This complex of barns, sheds, corrals, and employee housing was named Kenneyville to commemorate the firm's co-founder and his family of eight children. Today, a few tired-looking locust trees in the service yard of The Ahwahnee and a towering sequoia tree on the front lawn, planted by Kenney, are all that remain of the settlement of Kenneyville.

Until 1913, when automobiles were first readmitted into Yosemite Valley after a six-year ban, Kenneyville's equestrian population of horses, mules, donkeys, and ponies was huge, and the many varied vehicles ranged from lightweight buggies to cumbersome stages. Within a few years, automobiles were so practical and numerous that stables were needed only for pleasure-riding mounts and pack mules. Thus, Kenneyville's well-fertilized site, with its superb views of Half Dome, Glacier Point, and Yosemite Falls, would make, officials decided, a prime setting for the new hotel. Aside from Director Mather's reputed embarrassment at Lady Astor's disdain, there were valid reasons for a new guest facility to replace the ramshackle Sentinel Hotel.

Above: The aging Sentinel Hotel was the top accommodation in Yosemite until the construction of The Ahwahnee in 1927. Right: Don Tresidder, shown here with Mary Tresidder (daughter of Jennie and David Curry), worked his way up from porter at Camp Curry to president of the newly formed Yosemite Park & Curry Co. in 1925.

LUXURY ACCOMMODATIONS FOR A NEW ERA

By 1925, the Sentinel, the sole survivor of four early pioneer inns, consisted of seven deteriorating frame buildings and

The Ahwahnee Hotel

tents squeezed in among the boulders. Only the main building, literally overhanging the Merced River, was kept open in the winter. Moreover, its plumbing, heating, insulation, and rudimentary sewage system were inadequate to say the least. Winter visitation to Yosemite had never been large, as the old, unpaved roads were often blocked by snow and ice. By July 1926, however, completion of Highway 140, the All-Year Highway in the low-altitude Merced River Canyon, would eliminate seasonal isolation and increase travel. More and better accommodations were needed, and one of the clauses in a five-year contract between the National Park Service and the new Yosemite Park and Curry Co., signed in February 1925, called for a large fire-proof guest unit.

That agreement was negotiated only after Secretary of the Interior Hubert Work, Mather, and Albright had pressured the two leading competitive and combative Yosemite concessionaires into merging to become Yosemite Park and Curry Co. Dr. Donald B. Tresidder, 33 years old, who had abdicated the medical profession for innkeeping after marrying Jennie and David Curry's daughter Mary, was installed as president. Rutted, pioneer roads were being replaced by modern highways, and a new Park Service headquarters, museum, post office, and four photography shops were built in an attractive semi-circle on the sunny, north side of the valley. Guest housing was the next priority.

Jennie Curry (owner since 1899 of Camp Curry, a popular and

successful tent cabin accommodation beneath Glacier Point) objected to the idea of expensive accommodations in a place preserved for everyone to enjoy — rich or poor. But "Mother" Curry was overruled. Mather, whose very position as director of the new National Park Service was a result of influence, was familiar with the needs of the privileged. His determination to have a hostelry that would satisfy even the most fastidious guest was the driving force behind the push for a luxury hotel.

PLANNING THE NEW HOTEL

Mather, Secretary Work, W.B. Lewis, Superintendent of Yosemite National Park, and Tresidder were essential to its planning and development. Tresidder, by right of his position as president of

Top: Jennie and David Curry, with Jennie's father, Robert Foster, at Camp Curry, circa 1904. Above: NPS Director Stephen Mather (right) and NPS Chief Park Naturalist Ansel Hall with the model for the planned Yosemite Village.

furnish the hotel, and the company would operate it under a 20-year renewable contract, the government would own the land and structure, and the Park Service would set rates. At that time, YP&CCo. paid $5,000 a year for the privilege of operating in Yosemite and was allowed to make, if possible, six percent on its investment in Camp Curry, Yosemite Lodge, the general store, and the High Sierra Camps.

On April 13, 1925, less than two months after the merger, Work, Mather, Lewis, Albright, Tresidder, and several Curry Co. directors agreed upon Kenneyville as the site for the proposed new hotel. While cameras clicked, Secretary Work hammered in a symbolic cornerstake to mark the general placement of the proposed structure. After that, a new access road was staked out.

A new, much smaller stable, near what is presently known as North Pines Campground, was begun shortly thereafter. Directors of the Curry Co. planned to spend $300,000 for 100 bedrooms with baths. Satellite cottages would be built after the hotel's completion to supply 100 or more additional guest rooms. The 200 rooms, together with an enormous kitchen, cavernous dining room, and lobby in the main building, would be able to handle as many as 500 guests. Furthermore, the directors recommended that an Indian theme be used throughout the hotel and a topnotch architect hired.

GILBERT STANLEY UNDERWOOD

Harry Chandler investigated a Los Angeles-based architect

Yosemite Park and Curry Co., was the day-to-day decision-maker. Unfortunately, he had no building background and limited business experience. While attending college and medical school, he had sold cars, taught school briefly, and later worked his way up from porter to assistant manager at Camp Curry during the summers. As instant president, he was innovative, and like Mather, whom he admired, in a hurry. Inevitably, his leadership was affected by the actions and support of the new company's prestigious board of directors, which included A.B.C. (Alphabet) Dohrmann, an influential Bay Area entrepreneur who headed a hotel supply business, and Harry Chandler, publisher of the *Los Angeles Times*.

The Yosemite Park and Curry Co. was under the jurisdiction of the National Park Service to see that the public was served well at reasonable charges. Although company funds would build and named Gilbert Stanley Underwood who, at 35, headed his own firm. As consulting architect for the Union Pacific Railway, his specialty was large-scale terminals, but he was eager to work with the National Park Service. Through his friendship with two Park Service officials, he had come to the attention of Stephen Mather several years before and had been invited to submit plans for a new Yosemite Village development and post office. The plans for the village were rejected as too elaborate by officials. But, according to Park Historian William C. Tweed, Underwood's design for the post office was simplified and eventually constructed.

Underwood had earned his Masters in architecture at Yale and won two medals for design excellence. Biographer Joyce Zaitlin states that his early apprenticeship to Southern California architect Arthur Benton, well-known for his Southwestern Mission style of architecture, was also one of the reasons that Mather and the board of directors were particularly in favor of using him.

Some of the Curry Co. directors felt that Underwood lived too far away to give the job close supervision, but he told them that the Yosemite position offered him the opportunity of his life, and if necessary, he would move his entire office force to Yosemite. In July 1925, the directors retained him as architect for the new hotel for one year at a fee of $2,500 plus three percent commission on building costs. They instructed him to produce plans for a "hotel that fits the environment."

Opposite, top: Don Tresidder, president of Yosemite Park & Curry Co., gives an address at the cornerstone laying of the still-unnamed Ahwahnee on August 1, 1926. Behind him, from left to right, NPS Director Stephen Mather, A.B.C Dohrmann, and Jennie Curry. Opposite, bottom: The nightly Firefall at Camp Curry. This page, top: Gilbert Stanley Underwood, 1919. Above: Zion Lodge, Zion National Park, designed by Underwood for the Union Pacific Railroad in 1924.

CHAPTER II
Construction of The Ahwahnee

Underwood's preliminary plans showed a massive, six-story structure with three wings faced with native granite and concrete stained to look like redwood. Both the dining room and the Great Lounge were designed to be monumental: the former 130 feet long, 51 feet wide, and 34 feet high; the latter 77 feet long, 51 feet wide, and 24 feet high. Although the directors approved the exterior, they thought the interior, from an operating standpoint, was "incredibly bad." "To get from the kitchen to the service elevator," Tresidder pointed out, "meant passage through the long tunnel in the basement of some 100 feet in length." Another example of poor design, Tresidder wrote, was that Underwood planned rest rooms to open directly off the lobby "which, in view of modern hotel building, is almost impossible to believe." Back to the drawing board—only it took months of argument in letters, telephone calls, and confrontations, and finally, threats of discharge, before Underwood made changes enough to satisfy everyone.

It was late March 1926 before revised plans were approved by Mather who promised to be on hand for the official ground-breaking. Park Service laborers had been

working on the access road, and Curry Co. employees were building the new stables—Kenneyville still existed. Despite heavy rain on April 3 and 4, Curry Co. and Park Service dignitaries assembled on the site to watch the staking out of the rough dimensions of the enormous building. Shortly after the sodden ceremony, shops, structures, fences, hitching posts, and watering troughs at Kenneyville were razed. A couple of buildings were kept for storage of building materials. A Park Service crew removed nearby Public Camp No. 8 so that the lifestyles of campers and guests would not conflict.

Ordinarily, a contractor would not have been selected until construction bids had been advertised and the lowest bidder awarded the contract. On May 5, Tresidder advised the executive committee that to follow the usual procedure would take at least three months. Thus, actual construction would have to be delayed until almost winter. After considerable discussion, the directors agreed that haste was advisable and "this could best be accomplished by giving up the contract to a builder upon the basis of a guaranteed sum for the erection and completion."

THE RACE FOR COMPLETION

James L. McLaughlin, a San Francisco contractor who was reputed to be capable, reliable, and honest, was chosen. A native of Massachusetts, he had helped in San Francisco's reconstruction after the great earthquake of 1906. He had restored the old Mission Dolores Church, and later, built several schools, a

The Ahwahnee Hotel

seminary, and even a mausoleum, but only one small hotel in Chico, California. On June 2, after his conferences and investigations of the site and Underwood's 117-page specifications, McLaughlin promised in writing to build the structure "for a maximum guaranteed cost of $525,000, including our fee... on or before December 15, 1926." His proposal was accepted, and excavation for foundations begun immediately. McLaughlin had a cookhouse built and scores of tents set up to house the construction crew. Ultimately 245 laborers, carpenters, and skilled craftsmen worked on the hotel at different times.

Coincident with that, a San Francisco trucking firm, using six-wheel Fageol trucks, began hauling 1,000 tons of structural steel, 5,000 tons of building stone, $25,000 worth of kitchen equipment, and 60 percent of the furniture to the site. For 13 months, seven days a week, the haulage continued. According to the *Stockton Record*, "because of the variety and magnitude of the task ... [the project was] one of the most remarkable accomplishments in California automotive history. Included in the work ... was the hauling of 30,000 feet of logs from a timber stand near Big Oak Flat to the logging incline of the Yosemite Lumber Company (west of El Portal) over roads which... were unworthy of the name."

August 1, 1926 was set for the cornerstone laying of the still unnamed "Yosemite All-Year Hotel," as that date coincided with two days of Mather-prompted festivities revolving

around the official opening of the All-Year Highway from Merced to Yosemite Valley. A pageant, Indian contests, plaque unveilings, and dedication of the Happy Isles fish hatchery were other scheduled events. At 9:45 a.m., Jennie Curry and others spoke briefly at the cornerstone ceremony, watched by an audience of VIPs, including Stephen Mather. A surviving copy of the program states that "the new Yosemite All-Year Hotel will be completed by December 25, 1926, in time for a grand opening party over the Christmas and New Year's holidays.... With its furnishings, the Yosemite All-Year Hotel will cost approximately $800,000...it will have 100 rooms, all with baths, and will have ample accommodations for 1,000 diners...."

DISPUTES AND DELAYS

Promises, promises. The opening date turned out to be off by seven months, costs rose to a million dollars, and the vast dining room could seat only 350 people at one time. Inevitably,

Pages 18-19: Park Superintendent W.B. Lewis, A.B.C. Dohrmann, Tom Vint, Don Tresidder, and architect Gilbert Stanley Underwood proudly display the architectural plan for The Ahwahnee in 1925.

Opposite, top and bottom: Construction of The Ahwahnee began in April 1926. The transport of materials to the remote site was considered "one of the most remarkable accomplishments in California history" by the Stockton Record. *Above: The 34-foot-high vaulted dining room was supported by stripped sugar pine columns.*

21

Below: The mosaic floor in the entrance lobby. Bottom: Ansel Adams's photograph of one of the floor-to-ceiling windows in the Great Lounge.

there were delays due to weather and labor, but the chief fault lay with the obstructionist architect Underwood, as well as with Tresidder and the hierarchy of officials stirring the broth with ideas and changes. By mid-March 1927, builder McLaughlin exploded in a letter to Tresidder "... It is impossible to complete the construction... under the chaotic conditions created by the owners and their agents.... Already the changes in plans have made a structure so completely different in character that it is no longer within any contract we have with you.... The disorganization caused by the changes and the delays due to lack of decision, would raise the commission very much above the ordinary."

Underwood had not kept his promises; instead, he had caused endless problems by his stubbornness, absences, incomplete plans, and disloyalty to the Curry Co. After the foundations were partly in, Underwood decided a slightly different location would be more effective than the one chosen and approved. He tried to persuade the Park Service landscape engineer to order the change. Conversely, Underwood's supervisory architect, Perry Gage, was so competent that Tresidder offered him a position with the company. Gage declined at the time, but in 1939 became the company's superintendent of maintenance.

Even Mather and Albright were disgusted with Underwood's performance, and builder McLaughlin was seriously delayed because detailed drawings were not supplied to him in advance. Since the directors' views

on building were so divergent, Tresidder could not make prompt decisions. Their haste in selecting a builder was another fault, and certainly McLaughlin had erred in promising to complete the enormous, complicated building in less than six months. Local residents marveled at the structure's size, and the in-joke was that having failed to sell plans for a train station in Texas, Underwood had adapted them for the Yosemite hotel. Nevertheless, "Undie," who was a fast man with a quip, was popular with Valleyites.

NAMING THE HOTEL

Changes dictated by the directors and Tresidder added more than 18,000 square feet, at $5 per square foot, which culminated in further delay, disputes, confrontations, recriminations, and threats of lawsuits.

A signal mark of progress, however, was the naming of the hotel on October 12, 1926. After the customary "considerable discussion" of the executive committee, "Ahwahnee" was chosen as a dignified and suitable title. Presumably either Mary or Don Tresidder suggested Ahwahnee, as both were interested in Indian history and wanted the building to have a dominant Indian theme.

To achieve unique interior decoration, the company retained Drs. Phyllis Ackerman and Arthur Pope, a husband-and-wife team who were nationally-known art historians and experts. Their fee was $10,000. Dorothy Simpson was hired to prepare budgets and work with the experts as an associate consultant. Their job was complex, for they

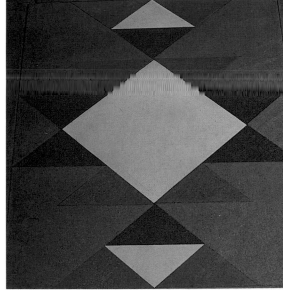

were responsible for everything from colors, furniture, silverware, linens, fabrics, lighting fixtures, carpets, and ornamentation to directing several young artists to do the tile, wood, metal, and plaster work. Interior work began about Christmas 1926 and continued until opening day, July 14, 1927.

Ornamentation, suggested by and adapted from patterns woven into Indian baskets, became the colorful theme of the building. Everything from the lobby floor, where six large geometric figures were set in striking rubber tile mosaics, to a vivid basket mural over the fireplace in the elevator lobby, narrow borders around the tops of the bedroom walls, and beautiful rugs carried out the Indian design forcefully and uniquely. The vast lounge was transformed into a friendly, welcoming place by a huge fireplace, comfortable furniture, handsome area rugs, and vigorous border designs on the ceiling beams. The hanging chandeliers combined a German Gothic design and Indian motifs.

According to George O'Bannon, editor of the *Oriental Rug Review*, there wasn't time to order large Navajo rugs to be woven by contract, so Ackerman and Pope, rug experts, ordered a total of 59 "kelims, soumaks, and other flatweaves from the Middle East": countries such as Turkey, Persia, Afghanistan, and Morocco. All were purchased from B. Altman and Co. of New York for $5,659. Prices ranged from a low of $48.75 to a high of $93.75. All were common patterns then and were chosen for their aesthetic value.

Top, left: The ceiling beams in the Great Lounge are decorated with brightly colored geometric designs inspired by Indian patterns. Top, right: Detail of the lobby floor's rubber-tile mosaics. Above: One of the superb antique rugs hanging in The Ahwahnee.

The Ahwahnee Hotel

Not only is that value far greater today, both artistically and monetarily, but, O'Bannon states, the remaining collection constitutes "a public treasure of Middle Eastern flatweave rugs." Present-day designer Marian Vantress and the Curry Co. deserve commendation for removing the rugs from storage and displaying them on walls in frames behind protective glass throughout The Ahwahnee. Regardless of Yosemite's natural wonders, O'Bannon says that "for rug aficionados, the kelims alone are worth the trip" [to The Ahwahnee]. This museum-caliber collection, he adds, "shows how oriental weavings and textiles can be used decoratively and that paintings, posters, and sculpture are not the only artistic creations which can satisfy an aesthetic and decorative need in living spaces."

DESIGN THEMES IN THE AHWAHNEE

One of the most striking features of the Great Lounge are 10 wide floor-to-ceiling windows, yet for months they equated disaster to Dr. Ackerman. In December, she had pronounced the already installed frames "execrable," and it was agreed that she and Pope submit designs for new frames so that Underwood could order replacements. In mid-March 1927, she discovered that because of "seriously negligent architectural administration" (on Underwood's part), the replacement frames had not even been ordered and further delay was impossible. Thus, she judged, the room was "irreparably damaged" unless "the one possible rendering solution can be introduced. This is stained glass for the top control panel. With that, the windows will take the place they should in the ensemble and the effect will be superb."

Once the directors agreed, young, intense Jeanette Dyer Spencer, who had studied stained glass design at the Louvre, was assigned as artist. Her full-sized designs incorporated motifs she had observed in Indian baskets. Each of the 10 five-by-six foot panels was different, yet harmonious, creating a room-banding frieze. In addition, Mrs. Spencer created the striking overmantel swirl of baskets mural in the elevator lobby, the ornamentation on the lounge's ceiling beams, and the Indian motifs throughout the hotel. Her work and dedication so impressed the Curry Co. that, after the Pope-Ackerman team left to found the Iranian Institute, she was employed as interior decorator for The Ahwahnee, thus assuring continuity of the original Indian decoration. Although elements of the Art Deco style, seen for example in the wrought-iron chandeliers in the dining room, were obvious, Indian ornamentation dominated throughout the building as a whole.

Not all of the public rooms were exclusively Indian in design. Three of the most notable exceptions were the writing room, the Colonial Sitting Room, and the California or Winter Club Room, which feature contrasting decors. An ornate mural, running the length of the wall, was painted by Robert Boardman Howard in the writing room. The mural

Opposite, top: The Winter Club Room. Opposite, bottom: Late afternoon light filters through the Great Lounge. This page, top: A closeup of one of the stained glass window designs by Jeannette Spencer. Above: One of the rustic wrought-iron lighting fixtures in The Ahwahnee.

mingles details of the plants, trees, and wildlife of Yosemite and is heavily influenced by the designs of William Morris and the British Arts and Crafts movement. Two themes dominate the California Room: the Gold Rush, as evidenced in old lithographs, wrought iron lamps, smoky lampshades, and heavy curtains, and a static but intriguing collec-tion of historical photographs, books, and trophies belonging to the Yosemite Winter Club, for which the room is headquarters. Corner fireplaces in these rooms add charm. The focus of the many-windowed solarium was a fountain fashioned from local jasper rock. Altogether, 14 public rooms for privacy and gatherings were incorporated into the ground and mezzanine floors. On the balcony at the south end of the Great Lounge, a smoking lounge and game room were built, while the mezzanine, over-looking the north end, contained a private dining room, beauty shop, and comfortable sitting area.

The dimensions of the dining room are even greater than those

of the Great Lounge, but its size subordinates to decor and views. Ten high windows on the south wall frame views of Glacier Point and attendant natural splendor, while the mammoth window in the alcove at the west affords a splendid view of Yosemite Falls. Colorful drapes are contrasted with golden-hued peeled log posts of eye-catching girth and a raftered ceiling. The solid log columns are barked sugar pine trees cut at historic Hazel Green, a former stage stop on the old Coulterville Road owned by Mrs. Curry. Adjoining the dining room, but unseen from it, is an immense kitchen, baking and butcher shops, store rooms, and walk-in freezers; the decor here is utilitarian rather than Indian, and the furnishings the most up-to-date available. In many ways, the shiny, sterile kitchen was (as it is today) the most important room in The Ahwahnee, for its culinary expertise would have an equally memorable effect on the hotel's guests as the hotel's splendid interior design.

Tresidder retained Swedish artist Gunnar Widforss, who specialized in watercolor paintings of America's national parks, to paint a series of exterior and interior pictures. One in particular was reproduced in many newspapers, others were used for menus and program covers, and several hang today in the hotel's lobby.

When it was possible to schedule a realistic date for the long-anticipated grand opening, July 16, 1927 was picked for the public opening, and July 14 for the private, complimentary celebration. Suddenly and belatedly,

officials realized that the noise from arriving and departing autos in the porte cochere to the east would disturb guests, especially at night, as bedrooms were directly above it. Tresidder gave an order for a completely new entrance on the north, with a covered walkway of 120 feet in length, to be built immediately. His right-hand man, Hil Oehlmann, recalled with amusement that "... with opening date set and the guests invited, the new construction was so hurriedly executed that it is only a slight exaggeration to state that the carpenters were only a few feet ahead of the painters, and the painters almost collided with the first arriving guests."

Opposite: The solarium catches light from three directions, making it a popular spot for reading and relaxing. Above: The dining room contains 10 floor-to-ceiling windows that offer diners breathtaking views of Yosemite Valley.

CHAPTER III

A Tradition is Born

Grandeur was inherent in every exterior and interior aspect of The Ahwahnee when it opened on the gala night of July 14, 1927. Chauffeured Cadillacs, Packards, and even a Rolls Royce or two deposited a complementary assemblage of California VIPs, including Curry Co. directors, Park Service officials, journalists, and politicians. They were welcomed by Don and Mary Tresidder, hotel manager Louise Temple, and uniformed staff members.

The "beautiful people" dined on stuffed squab, boned bass, and chicken quenelles. They imbibed water from Yosemite Valley's finest spring, listened to 11 speakers headed by Director Mather approving the hotel's elegance, and slept on linen sheets under hand-loomed blankets. All that and Half Dome too.

After the invitees left the next morning, the staff discovered a dismaying number of pewter ink stands, Indian baskets, and even bedspreads had gone with them. A day later, the first paying guests arrived, plunked down anywhere from $10 to $50 a day, American Plan—in contrast with the $4.50 and $7.50 top charges at Camp Curry and the Sentinel Hotel—and left with memories rather than mementos. Petty theft is still a

Previous page: Ansel Adams's photograph of The Ahwahnee captures the magic of its setting in Yosemite Valley.

The Ahwahnee originally contained a popular golf course; it was later removed to allow the grounds surrounding the hotel to return to the wild, in keeping with our modern understanding of fragile ecosystems. Photograph by Ansel Adams.

problem, but the first shocking rip-off has never been equalled.

"The Ahwahnee is designed quite frankly for people who know the delights of luxurious living and to whom the artistic elegance and the material comforts of their environment is important," boasted a promotional blurb. Lady Astor would have approved, but John Muir probably gyrated in his grave. Mother Curry refused to spend a night there, and, at least one critic expressed published irony, "...what a mistake to flaunt so boldly the luxury and profligacy of the millionaire class before the gaze of the unwashed thousands who come to Yosemite in their flivvers [popular slang for cars] to enjoy the simple life in the bosom of nature. Too big a contrast!

"Mr. Mather and the Department of the Interior should not have allowed such unbridled luxury in Yosemite. It causes the restless to be more restless."

A snooty doorman denied entrance to the coatless, tieless public, but complaints were few, and the affluent, well-dressed patrons enthusiastic. The first famous guest was Herbert Hoover, the first titled visitor Lord Wavertree, reportedly the second richest man in England. The first wedding at the hotel took place in August; the first convention in December; and the first Bracebridge Dinner on Christmas Day of 1928. However, leaks, cracks, and poor ventilation plagued the building. Repairs were made, but acrimony between architect Underwood and builder McLaughlin was renewed, and their threats of law suits against the Curry Co. for

delayed payment infuriated the executives. Eventually, compromises and payments calmed tempers, and Tresidder and Underwood, at least, reestablished rapport. That was lessened in 1928 when the North Rim Grand Canyon Lodge opened. It was obvious that Underwood had designed it to resemble The Ahwahnee's Rustic architecture. Later, his Sun Valley Lodge was also markedly similar.

THE BEST ... AT A PRICE

Despite good house counts, a Park Service official recorded that "The Ahwahnee lost nearly $75,000 in its first six months of operation....The preparation of food was particularly expensive, as they had imported chefs, specialty cooks, and altogether too many people....To control the cost, there was a big reduction in staff and a food controller brought in.... All trays were checked by him before being carried into the dining room. I jokingly accused him of counting the peas, and he admitted a close check because 'we've got to get the cost DOWN'."

Costs went up even further in 1928, as two tennis courts and the first seven of 24 planned cottages, containing 22 low-ceilinged bedrooms, were built. They were designed by Eldridge "Ted" Spencer, who had been selected to succeed talented, but unreliable, Underwood as the Curry Co. architect. Spencer, a graduate of the famed École des Beaux Arts in Paris and husband of Jeanette Spencer, designed attractive, ground-hugging structures with horizontal redwood siding and rough-textured shake roofs. Phyllis Ackerman continued the

Clockwise, from top: One of the cabins at The Ahwahnee, designed by Ted Spencer; these 1927 brochures touted the pleasures of the new "all-year" hotel; the Tresidders, who lived in the sixth-floor suite of The Ahwahnee, are seen here celebrating Stephen Mather's birthday in July 1928.

Top: The Depression years brought lean times to The Ahwahnee, exacerbated by a disastrous flood in 1937 that closed roads to the park. Above: Gertrude Stein approved of the emptiness of The Ahwahnee when she visited Yosemite in April 1935. Opposite: Dick Connett was manager of The Ahwahnee from 1942 to 1956—the longest tenure of any manager. From left to right: chef Fred Pierson, Connett, housekeeper Rose Crossley, dining room manager Karl Munson, chief clerk Charles Saul, and assistant manager Jack Curran.

Indian theme throughout the rooms, which were furnished with classic Colonial furniture. Unblemished wood paneling contrasted with the vivid Indian patterns on the inside and outside trim.

By then, Jeanette Spencer had succeeded Drs. Ackerman and Pope as interior designer, a post she retained for more than 40 years. During that same span, her husband continued as the Curry Co.'s architect. Their creativity, keyed to the environment, was to enhance all Yosemite Park and Curry Co. buildings, inside and out, until 1972.

The "Roaring Twenties" ended abruptly when the October 1929 stock market crash triggered the Great Depression of the 1930s. As the nation's economy plummeted, so did The Ahwahnee's house count. Within months, the exclusive hotel turned into a white elephant. No more cottages were built, staff and salaries were cut, yet patronage was so minis-

cule, particularly during the winter, that at times the Spencers, whose expenses were paid, were the sole guests. In 1933, when Yosemite's annual visitation dropped to 226,000 from a pre-Depression 450,000, total profit for all guest facilities from high country camps, stables, and gift shops, to The Ahwahnee, totaled only $1,495.

In April 1935, Gertrude Stein approved the emptiness. "We spent the night at the hotel. It was a very comfortable hotel and we ate very well. Nobody was there and it was a pleasant thing. We enjoyed everything. . . ." Not even the repeal of prohibition and the addition of a picturesque bar, replacing a no-longer-needed private dining room on the mezzanine, helped. Only five people were registered at The Ahwahnee in December 1937, when a disastrous flood damaged roads, bridges, trails, and some buildings. Nevertheless, in 1938, the national economy and the resultant patronage increased enough so that black ink replaced red on the Co.'s financial statements. Chauffeurs, limousines, and the snob atmosphere had become a rarity, however, and even campers, if well-dressed, were welcome in The Ahwahnee.

MANAGING THE AHWAHNEE

The hotel's first managers, Louise Temple and Dorothy Jacobson, were followed by a series of men: George Goldworthy, Howard Rossington, Earl Coffman, Jack Wentworth, and Ray Lillie. Dick Connett, who had trained under Mother Curry at Camp Curry, was appointed manager in 1942, and, with the

exception of service during World War II, served until 1956—the longest tenure of any manager before or since. The fifties, he said, were golden years when "pillow counts" regularly exceeded 200 and, during Christmas and Easter weeks, reached 260-270. "There were 142 staff members one post-war summer," Connett recalled, "including a tennis pro, a golf pro, wine stewards, and one attendant who did nothing but empty ash trays, turn lights off and on, and set up or take down card tables." Shades of the twenties!

Connett's staff including longtime chef Fred Pierson, housekeeper Rose Crossley, dining room manager Karl Munson, and perennial assistant manager Jack Curran, specialized in the attention to guests and details that made the operations of the hotel both smooth and successful. Of course, there were exceptions, such as the time Connett was observed chasing deer away from the wildflowers. When the guests objected to nocturnal visits from ring-tailed cats and raccoons, he had to order screens. Connett's duties extended to dealing with an eccentric woman guest who insisted on transplanting flowers from the Yosemite Lodge grounds to her cottage at The Ahwahnee.

Fashion plate Tony Tuason, a sybarite Filipino, and the Barrows, Bernadine and Carl, were such faithful annual returnees, they were considered family by the staff. Each year from 1947 to Carl Barrow's lamented death in 1985, the couple spent five summer weeks at the hotel, always in Room 417.

The Spencers spent so much time in The Ahwahnee that their small daughters referred to it as "My Wahnee." Many other repeat guests regarded it and Yosemite possessively, expecting and receiving the kind of personal service that is the hallmark of a great resort hotel.

A Royal Visit

Over the years since 1855, when Yosemite Valley first became a magnet for visitors, it has hosted and thrilled millions of people including many royal figures and 10 presidents of the United States.*

Yet, no visitation has inspired more excitement and preparation than that of the March 1983 visit of Her Majesty, Queen Elizabeth II, and His Royal Highness, Prince Philip, Duke of Edinburgh.

For months, the staffs of the National Park Service and the Yosemite Park and Curry Co. worked with the White House, the Secret Service, and the State Department to insure a smooth and safe three days for the couple and their entourage of 42. Unfortunately, the Queen's visit inspired such awful "British-style" weather that the royal route had to be changed, as two of the three highways leading into the valley were closed by storm-induced rock slides. Heavy rain was also a contributory factor in the tragic automobile accident that killed three Secret Service men in the escort party outside Yosemite.

Despite these complications, the low-key Yosemite schedule otherwise went smoothly from the royal arrival on March 5 until their departure on March 7. Park Superintendent Robert Binnew-

ies had a ho-hum-another-famous-guest feeling until he greeted the monarchs at Inspiration Point. That evaporated instantly upon meeting the composed and gracious Queen. Reflected Binnewies later, "There stood royalty, age, tradition. There was England, and I was awed."

Although many of Yosemite's spectacular landmarks were obscured by clouds, the Queen and the Prince were impressed and enthusiastic. As they turned to walk past the packed press box, Binnewies related that "the noise of 150 camera shutters was absolutely startling, prompting the Prince to remark he thought he would invest in Kodak Company stock."

So as to be fit for a queen, The Ahwahnee had been cleared of regular guests, and everything from floors to faces shone. Before the Queen entered, a "bomb-sniffer" dog prowled imperturbably through the impeccable rooms. The former Tresidder suite on the hotel's sixth floor had been suitably refurnished and repainted far enough in advance so there was no odor, a fact that drew a complimentary response from the Prince. Nothing had been overlooked by the nervous but excellent staff, who felt honored to be involved. Meals and

wines were superb. Special attention was also easing the situation for the anguished Secret Service comrades of the dead men. The proverbial stiff upper lip prevailed, regardless of the damp air outside. The Queen's physician took a long and (he said) splendid swim in the heated outdoor pool.

Royal activities were relaxed: a drive around the valley and a walk to the base of the rain-swollen Yosemite Falls. A special Sunday church service in the 1879 Yosemite Chapel was attended by the Queen, the Prince, a number of their party, and many local residents who had all undergone screening beforehand. (The ever-present canine bomb-sniffer performed his duty before the service.) That morning was singularly beautiful, for the sun, blue sky, and every snow-topped cliff were dazzling. By early afternoon, view-concealing clouds had returned.

Prince Philip's ready smile and affability charmed the attentive staff, but they also respected the Queen's reticence and aplomb. Her smiles were rare, yet could be radiant. Those privileged officials who dined at her alcove table—the Binnewieses, Curry Co. president Ed Hardy and his wife Jackie, U.S. Chief of Protocol Selwa Roosevelt and her husband Archibald, grandson of Teddy—

The Ahwahnee Hotel

were delighted with the animation and scope of the Queen's conversation. The Prince was particularly eloquent on the subject of conservation. And after he spilled wine on the pristine linen tablecloth, his "Oh, damn! I always do that" provoked laughter, as did other of his wry comments.

Before their departure on March 7, another rainy day, the Queen and the Prince gave private audiences in the Great Lounge to four couples. First, the Superintendent and his wife were given the royal couple's compliments and a framed color photograph of their majesties as a souvenir of the visit. Next, Ed Hardy and his wife were thanked for the unstinting hospitality and also given a photograph. Indicative of royal thoughtfulness, The Ahwahnee's manager, John

O'Neill, and his wife Karen were praised and presented with a picture, as was Chef Marinus de Bruin and his wife. The Prince added humor by exclaiming to O'Neill, "I say, I'll bet you will be glad to see the back of us!"

Undoubtedly, the Binnewies, Hardy, O'Neill, and their staffs were relieved that their immense responsibilities were almost over but not glad. Instead, they were proud that they had participated so successfully in a momentous occasion with such distinguished royal guests.

Longtime Curry Co. employee Martha Miller, who spent weeks as coordinator for the royal event, summed up the general opinion, saying, "The Queen's visit here was the ultimate experience. I never dreamed that I would have the chance or honor to serve her here in The Ahwahnee."

Queen Elizabeth II of England and Prince Philip, Duke of Edinburgh, brought British weather with them when they paid a two-day visit to Yosemite in March 1983.

A Tradition is Born

Celebrity Guests

Less than two weeks after The Ahwahnee's 1927 opening, Herbert Hoover checked in as The Ahwahnee's first celebrity guest. Although he was to return several times before and after his tenure as U.S. president, his initial visit was almost his last, because the disdainful doorman had to be persuaded to admit him when he returned from a fishing expedition in old clothes.

Both Dwight D. "Ike" Eisenhower and Ronald Reagan stayed at The Ahwahnee, but not during their terms as the nation's president. Only President John F. Kennedy did that while resting between two dam dedications in August 1962. Nothing was overlooked to ensure his safety and pleasure. President Kennedy's orthopedic bed was moved to The Ahwahnee; a White House switchboard was installed; all guests were evacuated from the second floor; an expert fisherman was assigned to catch trout; extra red fir bark was collected for a spectacular nightly Firefall from Glacier Point; and suspected Republican bears were chased

away. All three presidents were appreciative of the accommodation, services, and great natural surroundings. However, on an earlier sojourn, England's famous wartime prime minister Winston Churchill had been far less appreciative. "From what I recall of Mr. Churchill at that time," an executive remembered, "the kindest way to describe him is grumpy."

America's best-known First Lady, Eleanor Roosevelt, made friends while at The Ahwahnee, but also enjoyed roughing it in the high country, where she helped with the camp cooking and swam in frigid lake waters.

Will Rogers's visit and printed comments — "Everybody was apologizing for the fall as, on account of the Republicans giving us no more rains than they have, little water is coming over" — was a highlight of 1930. Poets such as Alfred Noyes, columnist Hedda Hopper, comedians, authors, generals, and many other celebrities have all been exposed to and thrilled with Yosemite as well as its classy, classic hotel.

From the beginning, Hollywood's biggest stars gave The Ahwahnee top billing. Most of them were on vacation, a few on location making films. Part of *The Caine Mutiny*, starring Van Johnson, Fred McMurray, José Ferrer, and Humphrey Bogart, was filmed in the hotel itself. Lucille Ball and husband Desi Arnaz were there twice: in 1947, filming part of *The Long, Long Trailer* in the park, and again in 1955, while making *Forever Darling*. Esther Williams, Van Johnson, and Wally Cox starred in a travelogue about the park. In 1988, the filming of *Star Trek IV*, partly set in Yosemite, drew crowds. Robert Redford, ex-Yosemite employee and producer of the widely acclaimed video, *Yosemite—The Fate of Heaven*, is a Yosemite and Ahwahnee devotee. Irene Dunne, Shirley Temple, John and Lionel Barrymore, Helen Hayes, Ginger Rogers, Boris Karloff, Yvonne DeCarlo, Alan Ladd, Adolph Menjou, Judy Garland, Frederick March, Clint Eastwood, and Charlton Heston have all "camped out" in

Opposite: President John F. Kennedy visited Yosemite in August 1962. This page, far left: Irene Dunne. Left: Boris Karloff. Bottom: President Herbert Hoover (far right) and his wife (second from left) visited The Ahwahnee in 1927. Here they pose with Don and Mary Tresidder (middle) and Superintendent W.B. Lewis (left).

The Ahwahnee. Kim Novak couldn't sleep until the bed was remade with her own purple sheets. Greta Garbo registered under an assumed name, but her trademark dark glasses and monogrammed luggage gave her away.

Comedian Jack Benny's visit was fondly remembered by staff and Yosemite residents because he visited the local elementary school, did some radio shows on his visits to the hotel, and contrary to his image, was a good tipper. Red Skelton was another favorite because he took and gave away photographs of delighted guests using the then newly developed Polaroid camera.

Singers whose voices were almost as majestic as the mountains have frequented Yosemite. Irish tenor John McCormack was one of the first to arrive at The Ahwahnee, soprano Anna Marie Alberghetti, one of the more recent. Marian Anderson's voice soared above Glacier Point for a televised show in 1959. Joan Sutherland went there on vacation, Jeanette McDonald on her honeymoon, and Lauritz Melchoir while making *The Thrill of Romance.*

Great Britain's Queen Elizabeth II was the most celebrated royal figure to stay at The Ahwahnee, but there have been other royal figures. King Baudouin of Belgium visited in 1959, and Queen Ratana of Nepal in 1960. In 1954, Emperor Haile Selassie and his 18-member staff, favorite elephant tusks, and 1,000 pounds of luggage invaded the hotel, and in 1960 the then-popular exiled Shah of Iran was given a standing ovation in the dining room. But not even royalty could equal the natural splendor of Yosemite.

*Kennedy, Taft, and both Theodore (Teddy) and Franklin Roosevelt visited Yosemite while in office; Grant, Garfield, Hayes, Hoover, Eisenhower, and Reagan came as private citizens.

CHAPTER IV
The Bracebridge Dinner

Lights dim, a gong sounds, horns blast, and the hum of conversation from expectant diners stills. The magic of another Bracebridge Dinner is beginning.

Rousing carols accompany the resplendently costumed Squire of Bracebridge Hall, his Lady, the Parson, and their retinue as they march regally down the aisle in the vast dining room to the raised table in the alcove at its end. After they are seated and the singers depart, the Housekeeper greets the Squire:

"A noble feast awaits thee, Lord,
The best my larder doth afford!"
"Thank thee, 'tis well!" The Squire booms his reply.
"Be seated all! I bid ye hail to Bracebridge Hall."

Next the tall, black-robed Parson speaks expansively:

"O welcome all!
Our honored Squire
Begs ye fulfill his high desire
That Lord and Lady, youth and maid
Give reign to mirth and not fade
The tumult of unceasing joy!"

A feast of food, song, pageant juggling, mirth, and delight follows that pronouncement. For nearly three

enchanted hours, the magic of creativity reigns. "The Bracebridge represents a Christmas that never was," says Andrea Fulton, its musical and stage director since 1979, "but a Christmas that lives in everyone's hearts."

Despite its high cost, ranging from $6 per person in 1940 to $120.58 in 1989, the Bracebridge is so popular that presently five performances, two on December 22, one on Christmas Eve, and two on Christmas Day, are given. A lottery has to be used to choose 1,800 guests from thousands of applicants. Knowledgeable old-timers have their applications for reservations in the Yosemite Post Office on the second Monday of January following each Bracebridge. To them, the fete is a beloved Christmas tradition, enhanced not dimmed by repe-

tition. Some people have returned again and again for nearly 50 years.

Don Tresidder, first president of Yosemite Park and Curry Co. delighted in festive occasions and wanted to mark The Ahwahnee's first Christmas with a suitable celebration. A special banquet with elaborate table decorations that he and his wife Mary helped to make was the result. Menus carried his message:

> This year with its first
> Christmas fire burning
> upon the hearth at The
> Ahwahnee, we hope that the
> spirit of the olden Christmas
> may find here an abiding
> place and that the warmth of
> our Yuletide cheer may be
> kept aglow in your hearts, to
> bring you back to welcome
> another Christmas in
> Yosemite.

THE ORIGIN OF THE BRACEBRIDGE

But the 1927 event was not dramatic enough so Tresidder hired Garnett Holme, a professional dramatist who had produced the popular "Ramona" pageant, to create a unique Christmas Day commemoration.

Originally, Bracebridge Hall, its genial Squire, and the Christmas celebration lived in an 1819 story by Washington Irving, better known as the author of *The Legend of Sleepy Hollow.* Holme based the initial Bracebridge on Irving's interpretation of a 17th-century Yorkshire festivity.

Don and Mary Tresidder portrayed the Squire and his Lady, who were flanked at the head table by a bewigged visiting Squire, his Lady, a Parson, and two others. All were VIPs, including Mother Curry herself. The

Housekeeper was Virginia Best Adams, whose husband Ansel Adams, a master of both camera and piano, played the Lord of Misrule. Local residents participated as the Villagers. An all-male chorus culled from San Francisco's prestigious Bohemian Club sang carols.

Despite mishaps occasioned by amateur actors, overly-spirited singers, and the spectacle of a very merry Adams climbing one of the 40-foot pillars, Holme predicted that the Bracebridge Dinner would become an annual event. With the unavoidable exceptions of floods that washed out one or two, and World War II, which cancelled four more, Bracebridge Dinners have been held every Christmas since 1928.*

Holme produced only the first, however, as he died a few weeks after its presentation. His successor was Ansel Adams, chosen because of his love for Yosemite, knowledge of music, and immense creativity. He searched out ancient, little-known carols and wrote vigorous text with a definite beat. It was Adams who instilled the enchanting quality that still makes the Bracebridge unique and unforgettable.

AN ANNUAL CHALLENGE

Jeannette Spencer, who had earlier created many of the beautiful interiors for The Ahwahnee, assumed the job of settings, decorations, and costuming.

*Opinions differ as to the year of the first Bracebridge. Most sources give 1927, but according to the YP&CCo. board of directors minutes, Holme produced the first one in 1928.

Pages 38-39: The Bracebridge Dinner, based on an 1819 story by Washington Irving, dramatizes the story of a banquet at the manor of Squire Bracebridge of Yorkshire, England. The popular dinner has been staged every Christmas since 1928. In this early scene, the Housekeeper sings, while the Squire and his entourage look on.

Opposite: Don and Mary Tresidder originated the roles of the Squire of Bracebridge Hall and his Lady. Above: Photographer Ansel Adams first played the Lord of Misrule. In 1929, Adams took over directing the Bracebridge Dinner after the death of Garnett Holme, its originator. Photographs by Ansel Adams.

Don Tresidder dubs the beef dish "Sir Loin, Baron of Beef." Photograph by Ansel Adams.

Many of her beautiful decorations are still in use. This talented duo continued their association with the Bracebridge until 1972 and 1973, respectively. In 1946, when the first post-war Bracebridge had to be planned on short notice, Adams asked Eugene Fulton, a longtime Bracebridge singer, voice teacher, and choral director, to assume the job of musical director, leaving Adams freer for overall direction. By then, his photographic work was so time-consuming, he needed annual assistance with the Bracebridge.

Two years later, another major change was caused by Don Tresidder's untimely death in January 1948. As Tresidder and Squire Bracebridge had been synonomous, it was suggested that the parts of the Squire and his family be eliminated. Responding promptly and negatively to this proposal, Adams argued that "not only would the total effect be seriously harmed, but I feel that the guests would react most unfavorably." A compromise was made, and from Christmas Day 1948 on, dramatists from the Bay Area filled the roles of the Squire, his Lady, the Parson, the House-keeper, and eventually, the Lord of Misrule. The traditional dinner (and the traditional loss of revenue) continued. Squire Tresidder would have approved.

Presently, Jill and George Willey are perfect in their portrayals of the Squire and his Lady. Geoffrey Lardner is a superb Parson. Since 1977, Edward C. Hardy, president of the Yosemite Park and Curry Co., has selected couples, often local residents, to take the non-speaking parts of the visiting Squire and his Lady. In 1979, Virginia and Ansel Adams were a happy choice. After nearly half a century of participation as Lord of Misrule, Major-Domo, photographer, and director, it must have seemed odd to him to passively survey the proceedings. Four years later, his son, Dr. Michael Adams, and his wife were seated at the head table. Afterwards, he said, "That was a great promotion for me. Once, years back, I was the Bear."

A NEW DIRECTOR

During his 32-year tenure, Fulton's combination of forceful personality and great musical expertise added further magic to the celebration. His charming and talented wife, Anna-Marie Fulton, became the piano accompanist and one of the singers. In time, both the Fulton daughters added their singing talents. Eugene Fulton's sudden death, after a dress rehearsal on Christmas Eve 1978, was devastating, but his family and cast rallied in the best "show must go on" spirit to produce, as they knew he would have wished, three more memorable Bracebridge performances. His daughter Andrea, whose part in the fete had ranged from a Villager at age five to the Minstrel, courageously took over directing the Bracebridge Singers. Only grieving staff and long-time guests were aware of the substitution.

In tribute to her considerable skills as a singer and leader, Andrea Fulton was appointed director the following year. Since then, her additions of song and text have been applauded. In tribute to her father, the Bracebridge Singers were renamed the Eugene Fulton Chorale. It is their hearty, robust voices raised in unison that provide the dramatic emotional atmosphere throughout the dinner. Few people can remain unmoved during the 14th-century "Angelus Ad Virginem" carol, or the stirring "Wassail Song."

Excepting the holiday season in Yosemite, when they present concerts in addition to the Bracebridge Dinners, choral group members work in various professions, mostly non-musical, in the San Francisco Bay Area. All are dedicated participants; some for as long as 35 years. They and their families are the guests of Yosemite Park and Curry Co.

Balance and artistry in both the choral effect and solos are supplied by 21 men and 16 women vocalists. Andrea Fulton and Jacqueline Victorino, in particular, are show stoppers.

A FOUR-COURSE BANQUET

The banquet, with its many courses, is heavy with symbolism. For example, the fish is historically associated with Christianity, whereas the boar's head, of pagan origin, signifies renunciation of animal sacrifice. Each of the dishes is represented by huge plaster simulations, borne by litter bearers and followed by the chorus, singing as they march. Each course is announced by the Parson and approved by the Squire. In the first presentation, the Parson says:

> "There comes, I see, a seemly dish—
> "Indeed, no other than the Fish!"

He is answered by the Squire,

Top: George Willey presently plays the Squire of Bracebridge. Above: Menu for the first Bracebridge Dinner, 1928.

44

Don Tresidder tries the flaming Wassail.
Photograph by Ansel Adams.

who lavishly sprinkles spices onto the papier mâché monster, exclaiming:

> *"A splendid fish! I'll add the*
> *relish!*
> *Sauce and citrus well*
> *embellish!"*

After that, a procession of waiters and waitresses trot in with trays held high to serve delectable fish with sauce and side dishes to applauding diners. While the fish is being consumed, the Housekeeper speaks:

> *"My Lord, a band of*
> *Villagers attend*
> *Thy door with song. Dost*
> *thou send*
> *Thy welcome?"*

His hearty response, *"Bid them to the Hall,"* results in a motley parade of folk, portrayed by Yosemite residents, and led by a white-shrouded man carrying a wooden effigy of a horse's skull. Its opening and closing jaws symbolize the Villagers' desire for

food, coin, or both.

The fish is followed by the Peacock Pie, a poultry delight. The main and most elaborate dish is the Baron of Beef. It is preceded by the Boar's Head and the singing of the traditional "Boar's Head Carole." The squire salutes it as:

> *"The bravest dish in all the*
> *land!*
> *Honored of old, I under-*
> *stand—*
> *Needless to dwell upon thy*
> *fame!"*

Almost immediately, succulent prime beef with side dishes, arrives, and the Squire continues:

> *"Another dish of ancient*
> *name*
> *Deserves high rank!"*

At that, the Squire takes a huge knife from the cook and says:

> *"With gesture brief I knight*
> *thee, Sir Loin,*
> *Baron of Beef!"*

In the intervals between

The Ahwahnee Hotel

courses, music, a lute player, and the antics of the Bear and the Lord of Misrule entertain the guests. Two solos, "Cantique de Noel" and "Green Groweth the Holly" are emotional highlights.

At last comes the announcement of the plum pudding and the Wassail by the Parson, whose accolade is:

> "Rich in every luscious
> detail
> Comes the Pudding and the
> Wassail!
> Merry men with buoyant
> song
> Bear the final course along!"

Before the Squire can respond, the Lord of Misrule cackles, "ZOUNDS! At last the Wassail goes the rounds!" That comment precedes the chorus singing their triumphal "Wass-heil! Wass-heil! Here's happiness to all" as the cast proceeds down the aisle one last time led by the Major Domo holding the flaming Wassail bowl above his head with both hands.

After a sip, the Squire approves:

> " 'Tis perfect!
> And I'm sure the flavor
> Shall inspire the most gay
> behavior!"

Soon the feast of food, music, and pageantry is over but not the pleasure of memory that lasts for years. Magic endures.

Top: The Eugene Fulton Chorale lend their voices to The Ahwahnee festivities. Above: The stately procession of the Squire of Bracebridge and his entourage through the dining hall.

The Bracebridge Dinner

Behind the
Bracebridge Scenes

Nothing is left to chance in the annual planning and execution of one of California's most famous dining spectacles. Reservation specialists spend the year organizing applicants, cancellations, and the coveted reservations for the five Bracebridge seatings. Martha Miller, manager of the Tuolumne Meadows Lodge during summers, is the coordinator and production manager, a job that involves the final weeks of intensive preparation. It requires all of her organizational abilities plus tact and graciousness to arrange seating for the 1,800 guests, some of whom are quite demanding.

Originally designed by Ted Spencer, the special head table set, including the Parson's pulpit, is removed from storage each year, as are Jeanette Spencer's stained glass roundells and other decorations. Carl Stephens, who has participated in the Bracebridge for more than 36 years, supervises their cleaning, repair, and installation, as well as seeing to the placement of fresh fruit on the litters and selecting greenery for the 12 large window garlands. For 18 years, Evelyn Christiansen, the costume designer and fitter, has kept the cast beautifully costumed, each one in dazzling color. Her job is pivotal to the production before, during, and after the five dinners.

The expertise and energies of The Ahwahnee's culinary staff, from executive chef to pot-washers, is crucial to successful Bracebridge Dinners. Changes in the menu are made only after exacting trial-and-tasting sessions. Food servers practice for their applauded entrances in unison at a jog trot. Wine stewards memorize the wine lists. Aching feet, backs, and heads are the inevitable aftermath, but so are satisfaction and pride.

There are numerous behind-the-scenes workers. In fact, every one of the hotel's 130 staff members contributes to creating the services and hospitality that epitomizes Bracebridge Hall, yesterday and today.

"Last, but not least," wrote Andrea Fulton in her 1983 *The Bracebridge Dinner* booklet, "the legions of appreciative guests are an integral part of Bracebridge, for their support and enthusiastic response is essential to the success of the performance."

As the Lord of Misrule might add, "AH-MEN!"

Opposite: Ansel Adams in his dual role as director and photographer of the Bracebridge Dinner. Above: Mary Tresidder (left) as the Squire's Lady with Don Tresidder's sister, Oliene.

The Bracebridge Dinner

CHAPTER V

Uncle Sam Moves In

W e train 'em. Statler gets 'em," was the wry comment of May Curry Tresidder, referring to the group of stylish hotels that often lured career-minded Ahwahnee employees away from the valley. But all that changed on December 7, 1941, the fateful day the Japanese bombed Pearl Harbor precipitating the United States' entry into World War II. From then on, Uncle Sam took 'em. Yosemite residents were far from exempt. Of the park's permanent population of roughly 1,000, 153 joined the services. Many others, including The Ahwahnee's manager, head bellman, and executive chef, moved away to go into war work.

Even Don Tresidder, the hotel's sixth-floor resident and Curry Co. president, the Squire of Bracebridge himself, was "drafted" by the trustees of Stanford University to serve as president of his alma mater. His right-hand man, Hil Oehlmann, was promptly appointed general manager of the Curry Co. Despite manifold problems with labor, supplies, and gas rationing, the company continued to serve guests, servicemen, and their wives throughout the war.

By 1942, Yosemite had been "invaded" by signal corpsmen who trained at Wawona and Badger Pass.

Previous page: The U.S. Navy arrived for a 2½-year stay at The Ahwahnee on June 23, 1943. The hotel was used as a convalescent hospital for the duration of World War II; 6,752 patients were treated.

Above: The navy built a number of out-buildings near The Ahwahnee, which were inherited by the Curry Co. after the war. Opposite: Everyone breathed a sign of relief when a men's club was built for recreation in the remote valley.

Moreover, 23,000 servicemen came to the park on leave for the rest and relaxation so inherent in its unparalleled environment. By war's end, August 14, 1945, that total had reached nearly 90,000 men and women. Not only did Uncle Sam take Yosemite's men and women, but its finest hotel as well! For all of its 16 years, the luxury hotel had been the bastion of famous guests: now, surprisingly, it was to be a beachhead for the U.S. Navy. Collectively, if not individually, the blue-clad sailors were heroes.

Admiral Edgar Woods, chief medical officer of the Twelfth Naval District, had been assigned the task of selecting a number of resort hotels to serve as convalescent hospitals to rehabilitate sick and injured men. One of his choices was The Ahwahnee. Tresidder and Woods worked out an agreement which resulted in the navy filing a condemnation suit, binding only during the war, and pledging $55,000 a year to pay for taxes, insurance, and depreciation on the hotel.

May 30, 1943 marked The Ahwahnee's last day for the duration as a civilian hotel, and Emily Lane, a Camp Curry employee since 1910, was a nostalgic eyewitness to its final hours. Afterwards, she described her feelings in a letter to her daughter.

I tried to go to dinner at The Ahwahnee but they had cleared out all food but enough for their 30 guests who must go after breakfast tomorrow morning. So I took the bus to the Lodge and after dinner there...I walked to the hotel, then walked slowly and sadly through all the [public] rooms, then sat up on the balcony, where the Bar is, swallowing hard and took in every comfy chair, beautiful rug, flower arrangement, and lamp to tuck away as fond memories. . . . I stayed on listening to the crackling of the huge log below [in the elevator lobby] until time for the Firefall. I found a nice deck chair outside between two full-blooming azaleas, heard the calls from Camp Curry and Glacier Point, proving how quiet is our Valley, and watched a not very full Firefall.

51

ENTERTAINING THE BOYS

If there was one thing on which officers and enlisted men concurred, it was hatred of the word "sheer." Sheer cliffs and sheer waterfalls were sheer horror.

"During this period," admitted an anonymous historian, "the hospital was literally saved by the people of the San Joaquin Valley . . . who provided recreational facilities of all kinds, brought hostesses and orchestras to the hospital for dances." But it wasn't until 1945 that regulations were changed, money infused, and adequate recreational facilities provided. The Ahwahnee grounds bristled with plywood structures containing a pool hall, a men's club, bowling alley, gymnastic equipment, wood-working room, rehabilitation center, and machine shop. These buildings were connected by covered pas-

sageways to one another and to The Ahwahnee, which bulked incongruously over its bastard flock. After April 25, 1945, beer could be purchased, at least at night, on the premises, and 1,000 to 1,500 pints were sold each night. Later, Captain Hayden reported, "No patient at this hospital has any real cause to complain of lack of recreation . . . Sufficient variety and amount is available to all."

Through the cooperation of the Curry Co. up to 90 housekeeping tents and 59 non-bath housekeeping cabins at Camp Curry, Camp 16, and Yosemite Lodge were rented very reasonably to the families of enlisted staff and patients. A number of housekeeping cabins with bath at the Lodge were rented by officers' families, again at reduced rates. Other

families lived in El Portal and pooled gas coupons and cars to travel back and forth to visit husbands and fathers.

The year 1945 marked the hospital's first, and last, really successful period in which patients were aided by physical, occupational, and educational services. During its nearly 30 months as a hospital, 6,752 patients were treated in The Ahwahnee. A patient load of 853 at a time, plus live-in staff, was not unusual, whereas a pre-war house count of 250 would have seemed excessive. World War II's end on August 15, 1945 presaged the hospital's demise exactly four months later. The Ahwahnee was not completely vacated until mid-January, however, and, after that, guarded by a crew of men from the Bureau of Yards and Docks.

58

TAKING OVER THE AHWAHNEE

The first sailor, a maintenance man, landed at The Ahwahnee on May 30, followed by a group of hospital corpsmen on June 7. Shortly afterwards, the first "battle" between the navy and the Curry Co. began. Sterling Cramer, chief accountant of the company, and John Loncaric of its hotel division, had the responsibility of inventorying and marking the furniture that was to be stored. As fast they would complete an inventory, pieces would be commandeered by the navy's commanding officer, Captain Edmiston, so the process had to be repeated. The navy kept the dining room furniture; some pieces were used by officers who lived in company houses, and the remainder, plus draperies, pictures, etc., was packed into railroad cars at El Portal for shipment to Oakland for storage. Unfortu-

nately, the Yosemite Valley Railway had a wreck on the run, seven cars went into the river, and the contents were damaged.

The second assault of the navy was destruction of the beautiful wildflower gardens, ruined by the construction of numerous temporary buildings on three sides of the hotel. On the fourth side, adjacent to the porte cochere, was the reflecting pool with encircling banks of wildflowers, which had been meticulously and expensively installed by Carl Purdy. According to Hil Oehlmann, that area too would have succumbed to the tidy, bare-ground standards of the navy had not Don Tresidder arrived at the spot just as a crew of workmen, armed with scrapers, picks, and shovels, prepared to do a thorough clean-up job. Tresidder was able to stop that depradation by talking to the men and their

commanding officer.

Inevitably, the character of the hotel was dramatically altered, irreparably so, local residents felt. A 76-page *History of the United States Naval Special Hospital, Yosemite National Park* factually documents the changes from the Great Lounge, which was turned into a dormitory for 350 men, to the Tresidders' "penthouse" on the sixth floor, which evolved into quarters for the commanding officers. The five guest rooms and two connecting balconies on the fifth floor were occupied by nurses, while the 19-bedroom fourth floor quartered sick officers. Second and third floors, with a total of 59 rooms, became wards although some rooms were used for labs, X-ray, and other medical purposes. Once again, the mezzanine bedrooms became offices. Five of the cottages were converted to wards, and the other three used as quarters for the hospital corps.

On the ground floor, the Sweet Shop turned into a commissary, the gift shop a personnel office, the cloak room outside the dining room, a post office, and the uncarpeted, drapeless dining room, a mess hall. The never used porte cochere at the east end of the building was closed in for storage. One of the most surprising room conversions was reported dryly by the navy history, and more colorfully by Hil Oehlmann, who is quoted below.

Before Admiral Woods selected The Ahwahnee as special Naval Hospital, he made a thorough examination of the building and premises. Naturally, he included the "Diggin's" in his survey and may even have sampled its alcoholic offerings once his official duties were complete.

A Captain Edmiston was the first commanding officer. His tenure was short for several reasons, one of which may have been his negative attitude toward Yosemite. After spending the first night in the valley, he expressed his personal distaste by remarking that he couldn't sleep because it was "too damn quiet." His successor was Captain Reynolds Hayden, a very devout Catholic, who soon concluded that the Diggin's would serve admirably as a chapel. So the bar was suitably adorned

with candles, a miniature replica of the Holy Family placed on one of the side tables, and all evidence of the room's former function was removed.

Six months later, Admiral Woods made an inspection trip to the hotel, and his first objective was the Diggin's to get a refreshing libation after his long journey from San Francisco. As he walked into the bar and observed its dramatically modified character, he almost exploded. He could only shout, "What a God-damned outrage. I had this place pegged for a proper officer's club!"

RELUCTANT RESIDENTS
On June 24, 1943, The Ahwahnee was commissioned as a special hospital for neuro-psychiatric patients. Sailors defined a psychoneurotic as "A man who has built a little world around himself in which the navy doesn't fit in." Neither did Yosemite Valley! Patients literally climbed the

Opposite: The Diggin's bar was originally earmarked to serve as an Officers Club by Admiral Woods; however, Captain Reynolds Hayden elected instead to cater to the souls of his charges and converted the room into a chapel. Above: A jeep perched precariously by Glacier Point during the war years.

53

54

walls, depressed rather than impressed by the granite cliffs. Sheer walls a prison made and claustrophobia rather than rehabilitation was the result.

An expensive, barbed-wire-topped steel fence was erected around the grounds, ostensibly to keep bear and deer out. Sailors got the message and commented, via a weekly newsheet, "Humanity would be better served if animals were locked inside and patients allowed out."

Even "out," patients were unhappy. Many of them felt that there was nothing but rocks and scenery, nothing to do. There

were few recreational facilities, no bars, though "green" beer could be bought at Degnan's Restaurant, and the nearest liberty "port" was Merced, 87 miles and a $5.75 bus fare away. Sailors felt isolated and forgotten. One likened the glacier-gouged valley to a titanic foxhole. Another said, "Yosemite is a beautiful place surrounded by solitude."

There is a right way and the navy way...Sailors were bussed to Badger Pass and set loose on the ski slopes—truly fish out of water. After five broken legs within two weeks, arrangements were made for a ski instructor.

It took a while, but the powers-that-be replaced the psychiatric cases with 900 medical and surgical patients, many of them combat veterans. Ambulatory men rode horseback, bicycled, and fished amid the grandeur and tranquility of Yosemite. Some became the "Romeos" of Camp Curry. For years, rangers in forest-green uniforms had signified romance for feminine guests. Now, "bell-bottomed trousers and coats of navy blue" captivated the gals. A number of romances led to weddings in the converted chapel.

Neither disability nor Yosemite

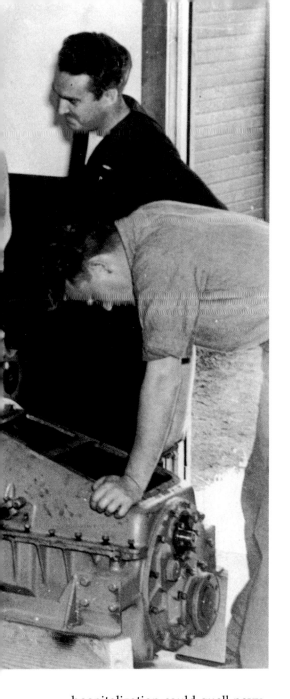

hospitalization could quell navy humor. One sailor requested a campaign ribbon because he had spent time "on the High Sea-eras." Another griped, "I joined the navy to fight Japs, not bears." A third suggested a permanent Firefall with the installation of red neon tubs mounted horizontally, ladder-like up the cliff to Glacier Point from the valley floor. These lights would glow all night, attracting mosquitoes, releasing men from gathering bark for the Firefall, and setting a course for sailors heading back to The Ahwahnee Hospital in the wee hours.

POSTWAR RENOVATION

Once the war, and gasoline rationing, were over, travel to Yosemite increased astoundingly. In 1946 visitation reached nearly 650,000, overtaxing accommodations. Reopening of The Ahwahnee To accommodate some of the crowd was a necessity, Hil Oehlmann told the navy, and as restoration would take months in which normal revenue would be nil, the navy should continue rental payments until December 1946. Finally, a compromise was reached wherein rental ceased on June 30, but restoration could begin on April 30, the date guards would be removed and the Yosemite Park and Curry Co. would again be responsible for the care and safeguarding of the premises.

"In lieu of restoration of the buildings and grounds, and the furniture, furnishings, and equipment now at the Hotel," Oehlmann wrote company directors on April 22, "the navy will pay us $175,700 and will deliver and transfer to us all buildings constructed by the navy on The Ahwahnee grounds...together with all fixtures and equipment therein." Most of the buildings were demolished after salvage of plumbing and electrical fixtures, valuable lumber, and other building materials. A few structures were moved elsewhere for use as storage, and one large building was moved and converted into a dormitory for women employees. The company was able to buy cash registers, air coolers, a floor polisher, and other surplus navy equipment. Later, in legal suits, the company won an increase in the three-year rental, plus a sub-

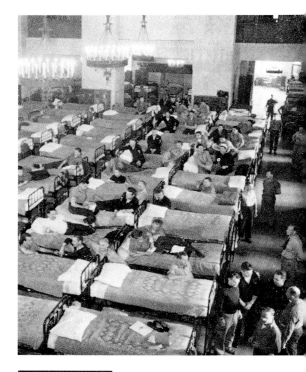

Opposite: Sailors turned to the machine shop for practical diversion. Above: The Great Lounge became Ward A. Sailors were, by and large, unappreciative of the magnificent beauty of Yosemite and longed for civilization.

22 rooms in them would be rented for the first time since May 1943. One cottage was reserved for the Spencer family. Daughter Frann, an artist, was helping with restoration too.

A general contractor and painting contractor were hired to clean, repair, paint, and recarpet the main building, a project complicated by the difficulty in getting materials and coordinating all phases. Reopening by Christmas seemed an impossibility, but the work force was large, hardworking, and dedicated. While temporary appendages were torn down outside, every room inside was scrubbed from floor to ceiling, plaster replaced, and built-in chests of drawers repaired. Sailors had banged holes in the walls, torn boards off closets, damaged the chests, and gouged floors. Plaster had been knocked off all the mighty pillars in the entrance lobby. About 80 percent of the rooms were repainted, and the other 20 percent scheduled for 1947.

Convalescing sailors in Yosemite shown beneath one of the giant sequoia trees in the park.

stantial damage settlement.

Restoration was directed by Jeannette and Ted Spencer, with the assistance of ex-serviceman Dick Connett, who was slated again to be The Ahwahnee's manager, and Rose Crossley, the able, silver-haired housekeeper. The Curry Co.'s maintenance department was in charge of repairing mechanical, electrical, and plumbing equipment in the main building and seven cottages, as well as the repair and cleaning of the latter. By August 7, Oehlmann reported, "practically all the work had been completed on the cottages," and the

UNDOING THE DAMAGE

What furniture had been left in the hotel was broken and scarred, and that returned from storage not much better because the damage from the train wreck had been improperly repaired. For example, spikes had been hammered into the 17th-century oak tables belonging in the Great Lounge. A furniture refinishing shop was set up in one of the navy buildings, and virtually every piece of furniture received attention in it. An enormous amount of reupholstering was done by outside firms, and other pieces cleaned in place. Most of the old, though not original, draperies were cleaned and re-hung. Small rugs were cleaned and mended, but new carpeting for hallways and guest rooms laid. By November 7, a Christmas season reopening looked feasible, even though major items, such as repainting the exterior, restoring gardens, walks, and the recreational areas, and removing the naval auditorium had not even begun. That same week, a quickly doused fire in the carpenter shop did more damage to nerves than furnishings.

Connett and Goldsworthy, who was in charge of the company's hotel division, signed up veterans Wendell Otter, Fred Pierson, and Miles Cooper as assistant manager, head chef, and head bellman, respectively, but had trouble hiring competent people for the many other jobs. Another returnee was transportation agent, popular Jack Curran, who had been in Yosemite since 1916, and on The Ahwahnee staff since its opening.

Presumably, Don Tresidder had a hand in the planning of the reopening, for like the July 14, 1927 grand opening, the first celebration was for the local residents, "those who have helped physically and spiritually with the job of restoring The Ahwahnee," reported the *Yosemite Sentinel*. For that one gala night, dancing and refreshments were on the house, and dinner only $2.25 plus tax. Besides the old, familiar, restored decor, residents saw some notable new decorative items. A large lamp made out of an Indian basket was a dominant feature of the entrance lobby, and an enormous,

geometric, over mantel design attracted all eyes in the Great Lounge. Talented Frann Spencer Reynolds, daughter of the proud and indispensable Spencers, had been the artist. Altogether, the interior design was as harmonious and unique as the original work directed by Drs. Ackerman and Pope; residents, many of whom had assisted in some way, applauded the finished work.

BACK TO PEACETIME

Next day, the first peacetime guests were warmly welcomed by the management and new staff, and on December 25, trumpet fanfare proclaimed the Bracebridge Dinner. The green light decision had not been made until mid-November, which left scant time for preparation. Both Jeannette Spencer, again in charge of sets, costumes, and decoration, and Ansel Adams, whose responsibility it was to recruit a cast and direct the performance, were under unusual pressure, and both reacted well. Because of wartime losses and changes, new props had to be made, electrical wiring redone, and even sheet music remade.

Afterwards, Adams judged, "It was a grand affair...gratifying beyond expectations." "I agree fully that the affair turned out very successfully," Oehlmann countered pragmatically, "but the high cost is quite disturbing...." A total of 215 guests had been served, but 67 of them were complimentary, and total revenue was only $1,601 versus the $3,250 expense. The charge for 1946 was $7.50 per person.

World War II was over, but the battle of the budget continued.

Jeannette Spencer painted this distinctive mural over the fireplace in the elevator lobby during restoration of The Ahwahnee.

57

CHAPTER VI
The Ahwahnee Today

Survival had to be the watchword of The Ahwahnee during the Great Depression and war years, flexibility ever since. The postwar decade brought increasing visitation to the park: 641,000 in 1946; more than a million in 1956; more than two million in 1967; and in excess of three million every year since 1987. Problems proliferated as people overtaxed facilities. Mission 66, the National Park Service's program to upgrade roads, buildings, and campgrounds, was implemented in the late fifties and later succeeded by a still-evolving General Management Plan in the eighties.

Because visitors need beds as well as beauty, Yosemite Park and Curry Co. concessions benefitted. Even the expensive Ahwahnee hotel enjoyed full house counts, except in winter. Dick Connett's lengthy tenure as manager ended in 1956; at this writing, a succession of 14 more men have now filled that position. All participated in the changes dictated by guests' needs and desires.

In 1950, a combined dancing, meeting, and cocktail place called the Indian Room was made out of the original porte cochere, which had been enclosed by the navy for storage. An extensive fire alarm system and unobtrusive exterior fire escape were other improvements of the

fifties. The elevator was automatized in 1963; and in 1964, the swimming pool was installed—a feat that was a good deal easier to accomplish than the installation of a 58-ton boulder as one of its "natural" features.

In earlier years, the elaborate three meals a day, provided with a room under the American Plan, had been the focus of the day for many lethargic, elderly guests. But that was too much for today's younger, more active, diet-and-exercise-conscious clientele. Lunch, which they had paid for, was often missed, as guests were off hiking, bicycling, or enjoying Yosemite in other diverse ways. Accordingly, The Ahwahnee switched to the European Plan in 1969.

A NEW ERA OF OWNERSHIP

Late in 1970, Mary Curry Tresidder died in her sixth-floor apartment, terminating the 71-year Curry family control that had already been weakened by Shasta Corporation's acquisition of a large block of stock in the Curry Co. in 1969. By 1971, U.S. Natural Resources, an even more aggressive concern, owned the Yosemite Park and Curry Co. During its two-year, new-broom-sweeps-clean reign, Hil Oehlmann, Stuart Cross, Jeannette and Ted Spencer, and many other experienced personnel were pressured to leave. In August 1973, MCA, Inc. (originally known as Music Corporation of America), an entertainment conglomerate, became the new owner, but surprised skeptics by retaining the Yosemite Park and Curry Co. name and what old-

Previous page: Arriving at the entrance to The Ahwahnee is like entering a country estate.

Above: The Indian Room bar opens out onto a patio area behind the hotel. Bottom: This closeup highlights the clever granite-and-stained-concrete construction of the hotel.

time staff was left. In time, it was realized that this new corporate owner from Hollywood (albeit supervised by the Park Service) was, in fact, responsive to both the environment and public concerns about the park, and willing to infuse large amounts of money to finance maintenance and improvement of all visitor facilities.

MCA executives wanted Edward C. Hardy, pragmatic vice president of the Los Angeles Athletic Club and manager of the Riviera Country Club, a vintage 1926 building, to be their chief operating officer in Yosemite. After a week-long survey of all the Curry units, Hardy, whose sensitivity to history was heightened by the Yosemite environment, accepted the job with the provision that massive funding be allocated for the rehabilitation of The Ahwahnee and other units. "I'm a snooper," Hardy remembers, "and because of my experience with the aging Riviera Club, well aware of the need for behind-the-scenes renovation. I found that The Ahwahnee needed new equipment, roofing, and overhaul so it would continue to be first-class in every way. MCA's Jay Stein enthusiastically agreed, and improvements have been

Top: The cozy elevator lobby and its attractive fireplace as seen from the staircase. Above: One of the pleasures of a winter visit to The Ahwahnee—relaxing in the warm solarium while snow lies on the ground outside.

The Ahwahnee Today

The Ahwahnee Hotel

The Ahwahnee today: the annual Chef's Holiday (top, far left); afternoon tea (middle left); rustic cabins with hand-hewn furniture (bottom left); winter fun in the snow (near left); and a perfect view of Half Dome from the patio of The Ahwahnee (above).

and are still being made."

In 1975 and 1976, for instance, every guest room window was replaced with a handsome new pane. Dark-framed screens were installed to foil the ring-tailed cats. Guests were delighted with the clearer views so long distorted by the old wavy glass. Another improvement we made," Hardy added, "was to replace all the old radiators with thermostatically controlled steam heaters." In anticipation of the 50th anniversary year, management budgeted $400,000 for a major program of improvement, including replacement of boilers, exterior renovation, and restoration of the interior decor.

A COMMITMENT TO EXCELLENCE

Attention to detail, always the hallmark of The Ahwahnee, continues. The nine-hole golf course and chain-link fence around the grounds were removed as no longer appropriate, but a wildflower trail was added. The 61-year-old porte cochere, built of logs two feet in circumference, had to be replaced. So did the hotel's slate roof. Each tile, weighing 1¼ pounds, needed to be installed and that took four years of work. In response to guest suggestions, television sets were installed in 1989, and air conditioning is planned for 1990.

Since 1976, Marian Vantress, a creative and sensitive interior designer, has been in charge of the remodeling and/or refurbishing of all Curry facilities. Her favorite, yet most difficult job because of the neglect and previous inappropriate choices, is the remodel of The Ahwahnee. Plans for colors, fabrics, furniture, and fixtures have to reflect the original Indian theme and have to receive approval from both Curry Co. and Park Service planners. "Seven major presentations were made," she explained "before final plans were accepted for the 1989 remodel of the 124 guest rooms, corridors, and cottages."

The result is a harmonious combination of Indian stencils reinforcing Jeannette Spencer's original friezes. Indirect lighting was added, as was hand-hewn English cottage furniture similar to that which the Tresidders had introduced in their former sixth-floor suite. "I don't think we'll ever be through renovation," Vantress admits. "It's a huge, challenging, but exciting job."

During the winter months, skiing vacationers have always been numerous and festive. In recent years, however, the Vintners' Holiday and the Chefs' Holiday events have become popular occasions, as wine tasting and gourmet meals, supervised by famed experts, vie with skis and snowshoes.

Although not as venerable as the 1879 pioneer hotel, The Wawona, a gracious wooden Victorian building situated at the south end of the park, The Ahwahnee has been a historic monument since 1977 and celebrated its 60th anniversary in 1987. It is not only classic but classy. Dedicated management, a multitude of services, and an unparalleled combination of beautiful decor and environment promise that The Ahwahnee will continue to be as enjoyable for present and future guests as it was for those of yesteryear.

63

In the 1920s, Swedish artist Gunnar "Weedy" Widforss divided his time between Grand Canyon and Yosemite. A number of his paintings hang in the lobby of The Ahwahnee Hotel. This exterior view of the hotel was painted shortly after it opened. (Detail of painting)